LET'S LEARN ABOUT MATH

LET'S SKIP COUNT

BY CRYSTAL SIKKENS

TABLE OF CONTENTS

A Crabtree Seedlings Book

Crabtree Publishing
crabtreebooks.com

School-to-Home Support for Caregivers and Teachers

This book helps children grow by letting them practice reading. Here are a few guiding questions to help the reader build comprehension skills. Possible answers appear here in red.

Before Reading:

- What do I know about skip counting?
  - *I know you skip numbers when you skip count.*
  - *I know skip counting is one way to count numbers and things.*
- What do I want to learn about skip counting?
  - *I want to learn how to skip count by twos.*
  - *I want to learn how to skip count by fives.*

During Reading:

- What have I learned so far?
  - *I have learned that skip counting by twos means you count every second number.*
  - *I have learned that you can skip count by any number other than one.*
- I wonder why...
  - *I wonder why you can't skip count by ones.*
  - *I wonder why 20 comes after 10 when skip counting by tens.*

After Reading:

- What did I learn about skip counting?
  - *I have learned that making groups helps me skip count.*
  - *I have learned that a hundreds chart can help me skip count.*
- Read the book again and look for the glossary words.
  - *I see the word **counting** on page 3 and the words **skip counting** on page 7. The other vocabulary words are found on pages 22 and 23.*

We are buying fruit with our mom. **Counting** helps us find out how many we have of each fruit.

We can count by ones.

We have 6 oranges.

We can also count by twos.

This is called **skip counting**. We came up with 8 apples counting by twos.

2 4 6 8

Skip counting helps me count faster.

1 2 3 4

I only had to count every second number.

5 **6** 7 **8**

We saw our neighbors at the store buying peppers.

Skip count by twos to find out how many they bought.

You can skip count by any number.

To skip count by fives, just count every fifth number.

1 2 3 4 **5**

6 7 8 9 **10**

11 12 13 14 **15**

Making **groups** helps us skip count.

Skip count by groups of 5 to count these grapes.

5 10

15 20 25

Skip counting by tens makes counting a large number of small items faster.

10

20

30

40

How many nuts did we buy?

Skip count by tens to find out.

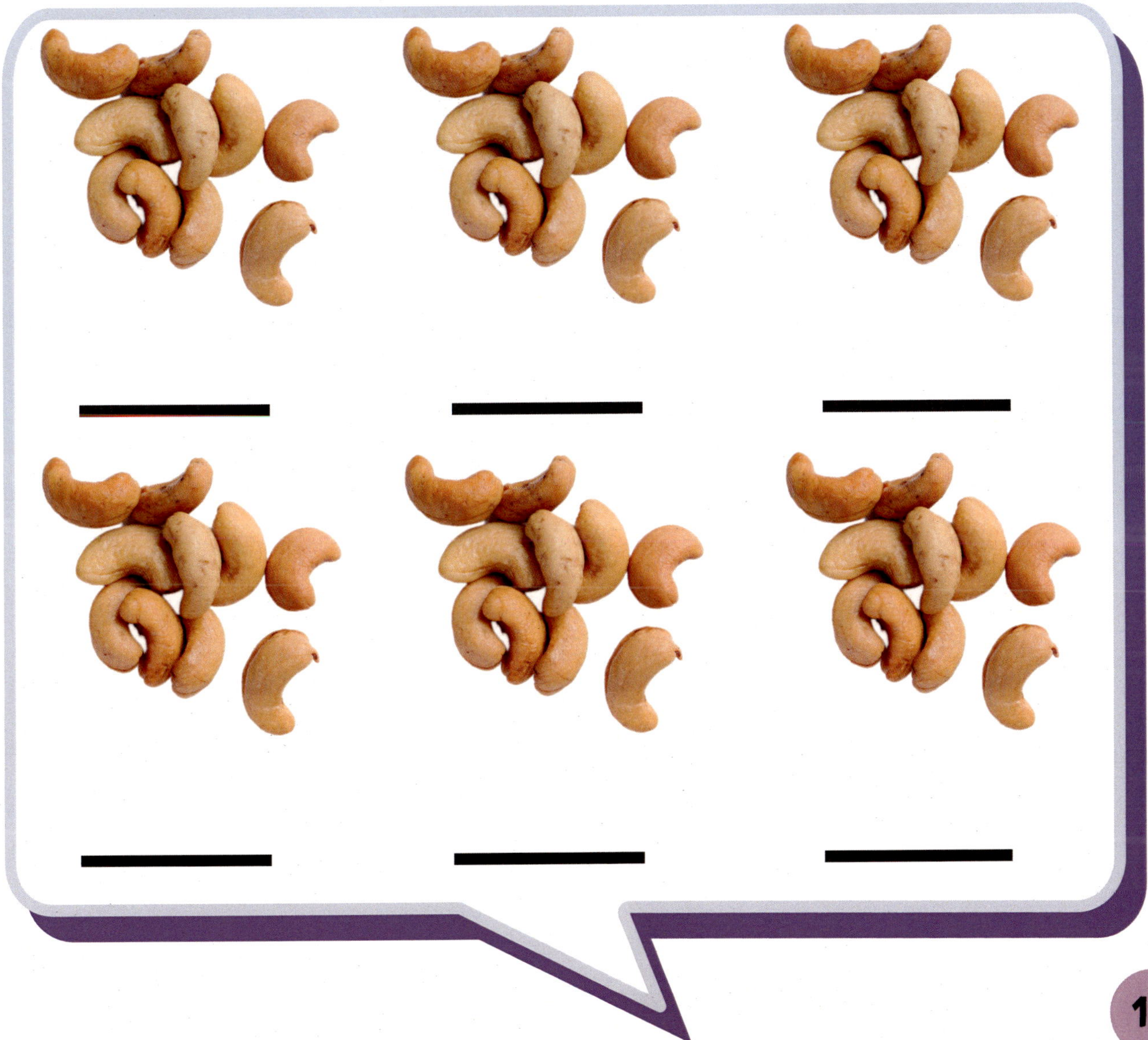

A **hundreds chart** can help us skip count by any number. What comes after 100 when skip counting by fives?

1	2	3	4	5	6	7	8	9	10
11	12	13	14	15	16	17	18	19	20
21	22	23	24	25	26	27	28	29	30
31	32	33	34	35	36	37	38	39	40
41	42	43	44	45	46	47	48	49	50
51	52	53	54	55	56	57	58	59	60
61	62	63	64	65	66	67	68	69	70
71	72	73	74	75	76	77	78	79	80
81	82	83	84	85	86	87	88	89	90
91	92	93	94	95	96	97	98	99	100

GLOSSARY

counting [kount-ing]: Adding to find the total number of objects in a group

groups [groops]: Similar things that are put together

hundreds chart [HUHNdrids chahrt]: A chart that shows the numbers 1 through 100

skip counting [skip kount-ing]: To count forward or backward by a number other than 1.

INDEX

ABOUT THE AUTHOR

Crystal Sikkens has been helping create books for Crabtree Publishing for over 20 years. In her spare time, she loves adding more animals to her family farm.

Written by: Crystal Sikkens
Editor: Kathy Middleton
Designed by: Samara Parent
Photographs: All images from Shutterstock
Production manager: Candice Campbell

Crabtree Publishing

crabtreebooks.com 800-387-7650

Hardcover: 978-1-0398-7276-9
Paperback: 978-1-0398-7334-6
Ebook (pdf): 978-1-0398-7390-2
Epub: 978-1-0398-7439-8

Published in Canada
Crabtree Publishing
616 Welland Avenue
St. Catharines, Ontario
L2M 5V6

Published in the United States
Crabtree Publishing
347 Fifth Avenue
Suite 1402-145
New York, New York, 10016

Library and Archives Canada Cataloguing in Publication
Available at Library and Archives Canada

Library of Congress Cataloging-in-Publication Data
Available at the Library of Congress

Printed in the U.S.A./CP032026